Name: _____

Handwriting Without Tears®

8001 MacArthur Blvd
Cabin John, MD 20818
301.263.2700
www.hwtears.com

Authors: Jan Z. Olsen, OTR and Edith H. Fine
Illustrator: Jef Mallett, creator of the *Frazz* comic strip
HWT Adviser: Emily F. Knapton, M.Ed., OTR/L
HWT Designers: Shannon Rutledge, Julie Koborg, Leah Connor, and Frances Nefsky
Additional Illustrations by: Jan Z. Olsen and Julie Olsen

Copyright © 2013 Handwriting Without Tears®

Third Edition
ISBN: 978-1-891627-74-3
123456789LSC191817
Printed in the U.S.A.

AUTHORS, ILLUSTRATOR, AND TEACHERS

Jan Z. Olsen, OTR

Jan is an occupational therapist. Her specialty is making it easy and fun for all students to learn handwriting. She originally developed the Handwriting Without Tears® program to help her own son. Now, the program helps millions of children. Jan is also an artist, but for this book, she and Edith thought Jef Mallett's cartoon characters were nifty.

Edith H. Fine

Edith loves words and writing. Her zany book *CryptoMania!* transports kids into Greek and Latin. She has co-authored two wildly popular grammar guides, *Nitty-Gritty Grammar* and *More Nitty Gritty Grammar*. Other award-winning books include *Under the Lemon Moon, Cricket at the Manger, Armando and the Blue Tarp School*, and *Water, Weed, and Wait*. www.edithfine.com

Jef Mallett

Jef is an award-winning cartoonist, as well as an author and pet lover. He started a daily comic strip when he was just 15-years-old. His *Frazz* comic strip was launched in 2001 and now runs in 200 newspapers. Jef is also the author of *Dangerous Dan*, a children's book.

Credit: Kim Kauffman Photography

Mr. Wright

zy Wright, a former otball player, coaches ursive like a pro.

Dr. Less

Maura Less writes spine-tingling mysteries. She is a stickler for grammar.

Mrs. New

Betty New speaks five languages. Besides English, she teaches Korean.

Mr. Case

Justin Case is new to teaching this year. His old car is always getting towed.

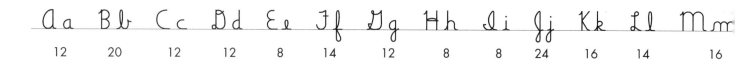
TABLE OF CONTENTS

INTRODUCTION

CURSIVE - **Fast and Neat**

CURSIVE & GRAMMAR - **Did she say Gramma?**

Mm Oo Pp Qq Rr Ss Tt Uu Vv Ww Xx Yy Zz

| 10 | 18 | 10 | 24 | 14 | 10 | 8 | 10 | 21 | 19 | 24 | 16 | 24 |

CURSIVE & GRAMMAR – Continued

CURSIVE WITH LATIN & GREEK – It's All Greek to Me!

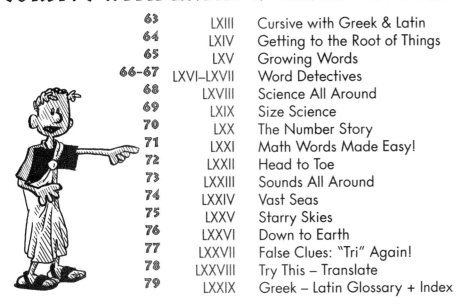

CURSIVE & THE WRITER'S NOTEBOOK

For Teachers

Can-Do Cursive - About this workbook

Can-Do Cursive is designed for fifth graders or older students at all cursive levels—from those who write cursive easily to those who know just a little. This workbook is also for you, a busy teacher who may not have been trained to teach handwriting. You can teach straight from this workbook. Just read this information, and stay a day ahead of your students as you follow the directions on each page.

What's Inside?

Can-Do Cursive is organized in four sections. The first section teaches and reviews cursive. The next three sections use cursive in fun, interesting ways to develop writing skills.

CURSIVE
Teach lowercase
letters and words.

GRAMMAR
Teach capitals, grammar,
and punctuation.

LATIN & GREEK
Build reading and
vocabulary skills.

WRITER'S NOTEBOOK
Teach a variety
of writing styles.

How do I use this book?

Start by teaching the first 42 pages in order. Those pages have the cursive handwriting lessons. After that, you may teach pages out of order to complement your other instruction. Some pages may take two or more days to complete. Plan to spend 10 to 15 minutes each day. There is no hurry.

What's In Style? This book uses a simple vertical style. This style is easy to learn and use. If your students have or develop a slanted style, that's fine. However, slanting is not a requirement.

Lines and Size This book is written with a letter size that is appropriate for students writing on regular ruled notebook paper. The first section, Cursive – Fast and Neat, uses a version of Handwriting Without Tears® double lines that has a solid black base line and just a faint gray mid line. It helps students make letters a consistent size and place tall, small, and descending letters correctly. After the first section, students write on single lines.

The FINE Print: A play on words with the co-author's name, Edith FINE, gives interesting information and tips. Sometimes the content is advanced instruction and sometimes it's just fun. Look for this bonus at the bottom of many pages.

 Extra Practice: Give students extra cursive practice outside the workbook. When you see this image, you'll find ideas for more writing activities. It's important that students use cursive once they've learned it.

For Teachers

How do I teach cursive?

It's as simple as demonstrating how to make the letters and teaching the connections (just follow the steps in the workbook). Connections can be confusing! This will help. Remember that when two letters are connected, the first letter is the boss of the connection. The first letter tells the second letter where to start. The second letter starts where the first letter ends.

Two Base Line Connections

Occur after 22 letters

- Base line to base line connection – easy

- Base line to high connection – tricky

Two High Connections

Occur after 4 letters – o, w, b, and v

- High to high connection – easy

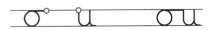

- High to low connection – tricky

What about capitals?

This workbook uses simple styles, but you may show other styles, too. Students often like to personalize the capitals for their signatures. That's fine. What about connecting them? Capitals are not always connected to the next letter. The workbook will say, "Connect" or "Do not connect." Remember that capitals connect only when it's easy, when the capital ends on the right side and on the base line.

Connect

Adam
Cindy

Do not connect

David
Pam

Teach and Check

Show students how to check their own and each other's work. The goal is for your whole class to write well. It is fine for them to check, coach, and help each other (see page 7 for further details). Here is what they check:

☑ **Check Letter**

1. Start correctly.
2. Do each step.
3. Bump the lines.

☑ **Check Word**

1. Make letters the right size.
2. Place letters correctly.
3. Connect letters correctly.

☑ **Check Sentence**

1. Start with a capital.
2. Put space between words.
3. Use punctuation.

Review and Mastery: Print to Cursive

After the cursive lessons, there is a translation activity on pages 26-27. Students translate printed letters and words into cursive. When you check those pages, you will see if there are any letters or connections that need to be reviewed. Have students use the page references for independent review, too.

pages 18–19	o	w	our	dog	was	now
	o	w	our	dog	was	now

For Students

Can-Do Cursive - About this workbook

This workbook is for you whether or not you know cursive. You can polish what you know and learn what you need. Knowing cursive is a real advantage. Cursive is faster to write and gives your writing an adult appearance. Cursive makes a good impression.

What's inside?

The first part of the book teaches or reviews cursive letters and words. After that, there are three more sections. In those sections, you'll use cursive as you learn other interesting things.

CURSIVE

GRAMMAR

LATIN & GREEK

WRITER'S NOTEBOOK

What's In Style? Can you read this?

In 1776, John Hancock signed the Declaration of Independence very large so that King George III of England would notice his signature.

Your parents and grandparents probably learned a style like this.

Thomas Edison, President Reagan, and President Clinton, used a simple vertical style.

Can-Do Cursive uses an efficient, vertical style — easy to learn, easy to write, and easy to read. If you prefer a fancier or slanted style, that's fine too.

The FINE Print   The expression, "Put your John Hancock on that," means sign your name.

For Students

Learn and Check
Learn letters, words, sentences, and how to check them.
When you see the box ☐, it's time to check your work.

☑ **Check letter** Teachers: Help children ✓ their letter for correct Start, Steps, and Bump.

Start correctly.   **2.** Do each step.   **3.** Bump the lines.

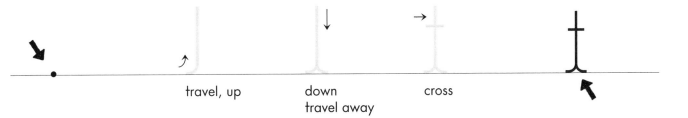

travel, up   down   cross
travel away

☑ **Check word** Teachers: Help children ✓ their word for correct letter Size, Placement, and Connections.

• Make letters the correct size.
• Place letters correctly - tall, small, or descending.   **3.** Connect letters correctly.

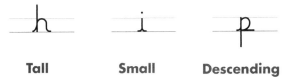   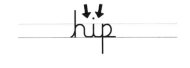

Tall   **Small**   **Descending**

☑ **Check sentence** Teachers: Help children ✓ their sentence for correct Capitalization,
Word Spacing, and Ending Punctuation.

• Start with a capital.   **2.** Put space between words.   **3.** End with . ? or !

CURSIVE - Fast and Neat

Mr. Wright

This is how to write cursive **t h e i**. Get ready . . . Now GO! GO! GO! GO!

t h e i

☑ Check Letter
1. Start correctly.
2. Do each step.
3. Bump the line.

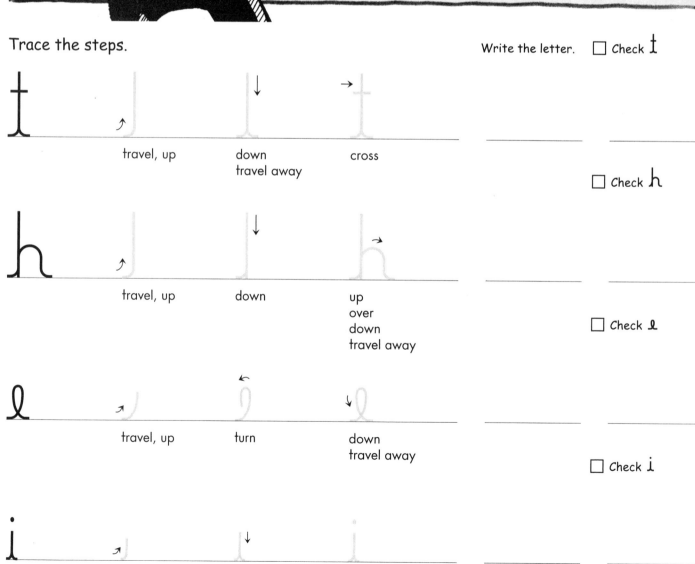

Trace the steps.

Write the letter. ☐ Check t

t
travel, up down cross
           travel away

h
travel, up down up
                  over
                  down
                  travel away

☐ Check h

☐ Check l

l
travel, up turn down
                  travel away

☐ Check i

i
travel, up down dot
           travel away

Copy the letters. Start on the dots.

t   t   t   t

h   h   h   h

l   l   l   l

i   i   i   i

This stuff is easy!
Cursive t h e i end on the baseline.
The next letter starts on the baseline.

☑ Check Word

1. Make letters the right size.
2. Place letters correctly.
3. Connect letters correctly.

Copy below the model.

Check the word.

t   the   tie   tee   the

                                           ☐ Check the

h   he   the   hit   he

                                           ☐ Check he

l   he   tee   tie   tee

                                           ☐ Check tee

i   it   the   hit   it

                                           ☐ Check it

The FINE Print   When one letter ends on the base line and the next letter starts on the base line, just travel away to connect!

Can-Do Cursive

Dr. Less

Did I tell you how much I lo-o-ove grammar? This is how to write cursive **p u n** and uh . . . uh . . . uh . . . oh yes, cursive **s**.

p u m s

☑ Check Letter
1. Start correctly.
2. Do each step.
3. Bump the lines.

Trace the steps.

Write the letter. ☐ Check p

p   travel, up   down   up   touch
                                        over   travel away
                                        around

☐ Check u

u   down   down
     travel   travel away
     up

☐ Check m

m   travel, up   up
     over   over
     down   down
                         travel away

☐ Check s

s   straight jet   make a J-turn   travel away
     takeoff   touch

Copy the letters. Start on the dots.

p   .   p   .   p   .   p   .

u   .   u   .   u   .   u   .

m   .   m   .   m   .   m   .

s   .   s   .   s   .   s   .

Grammar... I can't wait to teach you grammar.
But, let's do some cursive first.
Letter p is a descending letter.

☑ Check Word

1. Make letters the right size.
2. Place letters correctly.
3. Connect letters correctly.

Copy below the model.

Check the word.

p   pet   pie   tip   hip

                                          ☐ Check hip

u   put   hut   up   suit

                                          ☐ Check suit

m   in   pin   ten   pen

                                          ☐ Check pen

s   is   use   she   this

                                          ☐ Check this

The FINE Print   When one letter ends on the base line and the next letter starts on the base line, just travel away to connect!

This is how to write cursive **c**.
Now start **a**, **d**, **g** with the **c** stroke.

Mr. Case

c a d g

Trace the steps.   Write the letter. ☐ Check C

C   c

       print c
       travel away

                                                               ☐ Check a

a   c   c   c   a

       print c   up   touch   down
                                    travel away

                                                            ☐ Check d

d   c   c   d   d

       print c   up   up higher   down
                                    travel away

                                                            ☐ Check g

g   c   c   g   g

       print c   up   down   aim for corner
                    touch   turn   travel away

Copy the letters. Start on the dots.

c · c · c · c ·

a · a · a · a ·

d · d · d · d ·

g · g · g · g ·

Trace over each cc. Change the second c to make ca, cd, or cg.

cc   cc   cc   cc   cc

cc   cc   cc   cc   cc

Copy below the model.

c   cat   can   ice   cap

_____ _____ _____ _____ _____ ☐ Check cap

a   at   has   an   hat

_____ _____ _____ _____ _____ ☐ Check hat

d   did   had   said   pad

_____ _____ _____ _____ _____ ☐ Check pad

g   cage   gas   get   dig

_____ _____ _____ _____ _____ ☐ Check dig

This is how to write cursive r l f.

Trace the steps.

Write the letter. ☐ Check M

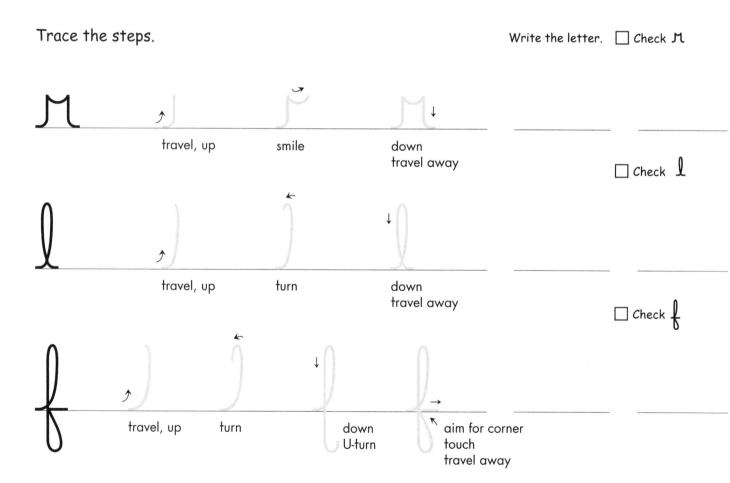

travel, up   smile   down
                               travel away

☐ Check l

travel, up   turn   down
                               travel away

☐ Check f

travel, up   turn   down   aim for corner
                      U-turn   touch
                                  travel away

Copy the letters. Start on the dots.

M . M . M . M .

l . l . l . l .

f . f . f . f .

Cursive f starts like cursive l.

Copy below the model.

Check the word.

r   run   their   her   are

☐ Check are

l   let   all   last   tell

☐ Check tell

f   if   after   find   first

☐ Check first

All right! Now let's do cursive **m**, **y**, and **k**.

Mr. Wright

m y k

Trace the steps.   Write the letter. ☐ Check m

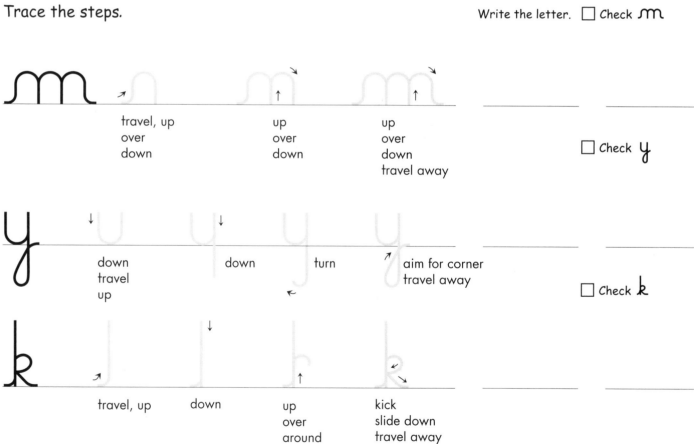

m

travel, up	up	up
over	over	over
down	down	down
		travel away

☐ Check y

y

down   down   turn   aim for corner
travel   travel away
up

☐ Check k

k

travel, up   down   up   kick
                        over   slide down
                        around   travel away

Copy the letters. Start on the dots.

m .   m .   m .   m .

y .   y .   y .   y .

k .   k .   k .   k .

No gaps in **m**, please!

Copy below the model.

Check the word.

m   me   him   them   mad

☐ Check mad

y   yes   my   say   pay

☐ Check pay

k   make   like   key   keep

☐ Check keep

My car gets towed all the time.
I know about tows.
Here are the Tow Truck Letters o, w, b, v.
They end with a tow!

TOW TRUCK LETTER

TOW

☑ Check Word
1. Make letters the right size.
2. Place letters correctly.
3. Connect letters correctly.

Trace the steps.

Write the letter. ☐ Check 𝑜

print c   circle around   end with a tow

Copy the letters. Start on the dot.

𝑜   •   𝑜   •   𝑜   •   𝑜   •

Copy below the model.

ou	our	out	four

☐ Check four

oa	oat	road	soap

☐ Check soap

od	code	soda	pod

☐ Check pod

og	dog	fog	frog

☐ Check frog

The FINE Print   The Tow Truck Letters **o, w, b, v** are the only lowercase letters that do not end on the base line.

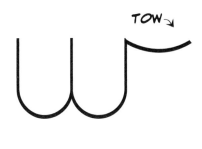

TOW

Trace the steps.

Write the letter. ☐ Check ⅏

↓ ⅏   ↓ ⅏   ⅏

down   down   end with a tow
travel, up   travel, up

Copy the letters. Start on the dot.

⅏ •   ⅏ •   ⅏ •   ⅏ •

Copy below the model.

wo   wood   two   would

☐ Check would

wa   was   way   want

☐ Check want

ow   now   how   glow

☐ Check glow

aw   saw   paw   draw

☐ Check draw

TOW TRUCK LETTER

TOW

Trace the steps.

Write the letter. ☐ Check *b*

b   *b*   *b*   *b*

start with an *l*   travel up   end with a tow

Copy the letters. Start on the dot.

b .   *b* .   *b* .   *b* .

Copy below the model.

ba	*bad*	*band*	*back*

☐ Check *back*

bu	*but*	*build*	*bunch*

☐ Check *bunc*

by	*bye*	*baby*	*byte*

☐ Check *byte*

bo	*boat*	*body*	*about*

☐ Check *about*

TOW TRUCK LETTER

Trace the steps.   Write the letter. ☐ Check V͡

slide down   up   end with a tow

Copy the letters. Start on the dot.

V   ⋅   V   ⋅   V   ⋅   V   ⋅

Copy below the model.

va   vase   value   oval

                                                    ☐ Check oval

vo   vow   vocal   voyage

                                                    ☐ Check voyage

vu   vulture   vulgar   divulge

                                                    ☐ Check divulge

CRANKED UP TO TOW

You can't tow these letters unless you crank them up.

t   h   k   n   p   m

Crank up the start of the letters! They look like this cranked up.

t   h   k   n   p   m

Copy below the model.

t → t   got   vote   boot

h → h   why   when   what

k → k   look   joke   book

n → n   on   one   own

p → p   pop   stop   hope

m → m   home   some   dome

CRANKED UP TO TOW

It's the same story for these letters.

e   l   f   i   r   s

Crank up the start of the letters! They look like this cranked up.

e   l   f   i   r   s

Copy below the model.

e → e	be	over	have
l → l	old	owl	blue
f → f	of	off	often
i → i	with	big	virus
r → r	or	for	more
s → s	most	lost	boss

Trace the steps.

Write the letter ☐ Check *j*

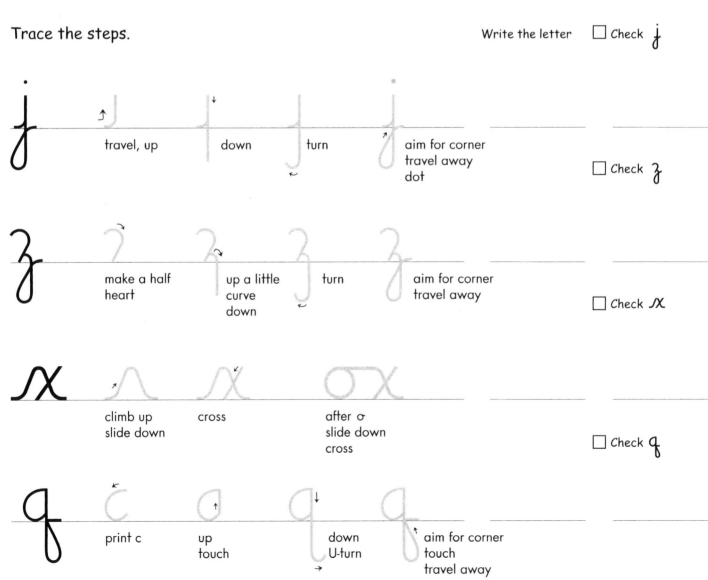

j — travel, up | down | turn | aim for corner / travel away / dot

☐ Check *z*

z — make a half heart | up a little curve down | turn | aim for corner / travel away

☐ Check *x*

x — climb up slide down | cross | after o slide down cross

☐ Check *q*

q — print c | up touch | down U-turn | aim for corner touch travel away

Copy the letters. Start on the dots.

j · j · j · j ·

z · z · z · z ·

x · x · x · x ·

q · q · q · q ·

Check the word.

j   just   jump   jar

☐ Check jar

z   zoo   zero   froze

☐ Check froze

lazy   pizza   jazz

☐ Check jazz

x   six   tax   box

☐ Check box

q   quit   equal   quick

☐ Check quick

Review & Mastery: Print to Cursive

Translate — Not Spanish, French, or Chinese.
You will translate print into cursive.

Translate print into cursive. Write below the models. If you need help, see the lesson pages.

pages 8–9
t   h   e   i   the   it

pages 10–11
p   u   n   s   put   in   is

pages 12–13
c   a   d   g   cat   had   dig

pages 14–15
r   l   f   run   let   if

pages 16–17
m   y   k   make   yes   key

The FINE Print   Check cat, had, dig to be sure a, d, g start with cursive c.

Translate print into cursive. Write below the models. If you need help, see the lesson pages.

pages
18–19   o   w   our   dog   was   now

pages
20–21   b   v   but   by   vase   vow

page
22   got   why   look   on   pop   home

page
23   be   old   of   with   for   most

Finish!

pages
24–25   j   z   x   q   jar   zero   six   quit

The FINE Print   Teachers and students, check these pages. Brush up on any needed letters or words.

CURSIVE & GRAMMAR - Did she say Gramma?

START CAPITALS

You may use P R I N T E D capitals until you learn C U R S I V E capitals.
Can-Do Cursive teaches these capitals, but you may use other styles.

a B C D E F G H I J K L M

N O P Q R S J U V W X Y Z

START GRAMMAR

Gr**a**mm**a**r has two **a**'s, just like Gr**a**mm**a**! The rules for speaking and writing a language are called grammar. Here are some basic grammar rules.

1. A sentence expresses a complete thought. **I write words.**
2. Sentences have two parts: the subject and the predicate.
   • The subject "**I**" tells who or what the sentence is about.
   • The predicate "**write words**" tells what the subject is or what the subject is doing.
3. Sentences start with capital letters.
4. Sentences stop with a **.** **!** or **?**

EIGHT PARTS OF SPEECH

WORDS AND THEIR JOBS – EIGHT PARTS OF SPEECH

Words work. They have jobs. There are eight jobs. Here is a fun way to learn how words work.

1. Nouns — give you a <u>name</u>.

2. Adjectives — make you <u>smart</u> and <u>good looking</u>.

3. Pronouns — let <u>you</u> talk about <u>yourself</u>. "<u>I</u> am the <u>one</u>. Look at <u>me</u>."

4. Verbs — <u>make</u> you what you <u>are</u>. Verbs also <u>make</u> you <u>run</u> and <u>think</u>.

5. Adverbs — help you run <u>quickly</u>, and <u>always</u> think <u>brilliantly</u>.

6. Prepositions — put you <u>before</u> other people, <u>on</u> top <u>of</u> the world.

7. Conjunctions — put this <u>and</u> that together, <u>or</u> apart, <u>but</u> it's your choice.

8. Interjections — say, "<u>Gee whiz</u>!"

PARTS OF SPEECH

Below are some examples. Now, you write two more.

1. Nouns   bus   man   _____   _____
2. Adjectives   large   young   _____   _____
3. Pronouns   she   they   _____   _____
4. Verbs   write   run   _____   _____
5. Adverbs   slowly   never   _____   _____
6. Prepositions   in   under   _____   _____
7. Conjunctions   or   _____   _____
8. Interjections Oh no!   Golly!   _____   _____

The FINE Print   Here is another way to learn how words work. **It is the eight parts of speech.**

1. <u>Nouns</u>   name people, places, things, or ideas.
2. <u>Adjectives</u>   describe nouns or pronouns.
3. <u>Pronouns</u>   take the place of nouns.
4. <u>Verbs</u>   show actions or state of being.
5. <u>Adverbs</u>   describe verbs, adjectives, or other adverbs.
6. <u>Prepositions</u> show position in time or space.
7. <u>Conjunctions</u> join words or groups of words.
8. <u>Interjections</u> show emotion with one or two words.

WORDS WORK

ONE WORD CAN DO DIFFERENT JOBS
Words are amazing. They can do many different jobs. Take the word, "paint."

I paint. — Paint is a verb.

yellow paint — Paint is a common noun.

The pony's name is Paint. — Paint is a proper noun.

WORDS CAN CHANGE CLOTHES TO DO OTHER JOBS
Words can change. They can even get help to do more jobs.

Take paint and add -ed = painted. Write painted on the lines in cursive.

a _____ door — Painted is an adjective.

I _____ . — Painted is a past tense verb.

I have _____ all day. — With helping "have," painted is a perfect verb.

Take paint and add -ing = painting. Write painting on the lines in cursive.

a _____ of a dog — Painting is a noun.

a _____ lesson — Painting is an adjective.

I am _____ . — With helping "am," painting is a verb.

WORDS AGREE WITH EACH OTHER
Subjects and verbs must agree. Write the right verb: am are is

I _____ . You _____ . Joshua _____ . She _____

Subjects and verbs must agree. Write the right verb: run runs

I _____ . You _____ . He _____ . Maya _____ .

STARTING AND STOPPING PUNCTUATION . ? !

STARTING AND STOPPING PUNCTUATION . ? !
Start sentences with a capital.
Stop with a period, exclamation point, or question mark.

SENTENCE TYPES

1. Declarative sentences make a statement. They end with a period.
Make up an ending to the sentence. Stop with a period.

An ambulance

2. Interrogative sentences ask a question. They end with a question mark.
Make up endings to the questions. Stop with a question mark.

Who

What

When

Where

3. Exclamatory sentences show strong emotion. They end with an exclamation point.
Copy these exclamations. Stop with an exclamation point.

Watch out for the snake! *A snake is loose!*

4. Imperative sentences are bossy. They make a request or give an order. They end with a period
or exclamation point.
Copy the imperative sentence. Stop with an exclamation point.

Call an ambulance!

☑ Check Sentence
1. Start with a capital.
2. Put space between words.
3. Use punctuation.

☐ Check Sentence

The FINE Print   Sometimes a subject is missing from a sentence, but you can figure it out. "Watch out!" means "**You** watch out."
In England, a period is called a full stop.

COMMON NOUNS

people, places, things

If you can picture something, it's usually a **noun**.
Common nouns name people, places, or things.
Proper nouns name specific people, places, or things.

Draw a person, maybe a teacher.	Draw a place, maybe a beach.	Draw a thing, maybe an easy chair.

PEOPLE   **PLACES**   **THINGS**

Copy these common nouns below the models.

PEOPLE	PLACES	THINGS
artist	apartment	apron
clown	city	chair
usher	universe	umbrella
yodeler	yard	yo-yo
zoologist	zoo	zebra

The FINE Print   Writing lowercase a, c, u, y, and z will get you ready for capital a, c, u, y, and z on the next page.

32 *Can-Do Cursive*   © 2013 Handwriting Without Tears®

PROPER NOUNS

CAPITALS
A C U Y Z

EASY CAPITALS

These capitals are easy. They are like the lowercase letters.
Copy the capitals. Connect them to the lowercase letters.

Aa _____ Aa _____ Aa _____ ☐ Check Aa

Cc _____ Cc _____ Cc _____ ☐ Check Cc

Uu _____ Uu _____ Uu _____ ☐ Check Uu

Yy _____ Yy _____ Yy _____ ☐ Check Yy

Zz _____ Zz _____ Zz _____ ☐ Check Zz

PROPER NOUNS

Names of specific places are proper nouns.
Copy below the models. Start with a capital.

Alaska   Africa   Asia

Cairo   Canada   China

Ukraine   Uruguay   Utah

Yukon   Yemen   Yalta

Zaire   Zambia   Zimbabwe

Write sentences about places that start with A, C, U, Y, and Z.

PROPER NOUNS

CAPITALS
O V W X

Here are more easy capitals.
Copy the capitals. Do not connect them.

Oo   Oo   Oo   ☐ Check O o

Vv   Vv   Vv   ☐ Check V v

Ww   Ww   Ww   ☐ Check W w

Xx   Xx   Xx   ☐ Check X x

PROPER NOUNS

Names of specific people are proper nouns.
Copy below the models. Start with a capital.

Owen   Olivia   Oscar

Vincent   Victoria   Valerie

William   Wendy   Winston

Xavier   Xenia   Xandy

Draw a picture of what you imagine Owen and Valerie look like.

Owen	Valerie

Trace the steps and write.

J   ′   J   J   ☐ Check J
   ready (big)   down   J-turn

J   ′   J   J   J   ☐ Check J
   ready (big)   down   J-turn   cross

P   ′   1   P   ☐ Check P
   ready   down   up, over, around

B   ′   1   P   B   ☐ Check B
   ready   down   up, over, around   around again

R   ′   1   P   R   ☐ Check R
   ready   down   up, over, around   slide down travel away

M   ′   1   n   M   ☐ Check M
   ready   down   up, over down   one more travel away

N   ′   1   N   ☐ Check N
   ready   down   up, over down

K   ′   1   K   K   ☐ Check K
   ready   down   kick   slide down travel away

Copy below the models. Do not connect the letters.

Jt   Jf   Pp   Bb

Copy the capitals. Connect them to the lowercase letters.

Rr   Mm   Nn   Kk

The FINE Print   Are you wondering about connecting capital letters? They do not always connect to the next letter. Only connect if the capital ends on the right side and on the base line. On this page, capitals **R**, **M**, **N**, **K** are the capitals that connect.

VERBS PRESENT (Tense)
I <u>talk</u>. She <u>talks</u>.

CAPITAL
S

Verbs show action.   **talk**
Verbs show tense.   **I talk.** (present tense = now)
Verbs agree with subjects. **I talk. She talks.**

Trace the steps.   Write the letter.   ☐ Check *S*

S / S S

slide up   print S   end

Copy **She**. Do not connect **S** to the next letter.
Write sentences. Make the verbs agree. Add **-s.**

I talk.   *She talks.*

I listen.

I smile.

I grin.

I wonder.

Copy **Sarah** or write another name that starts with **S**.
Write sentences. Make the verbs agree. Add **-es** because the verb ends in **ch**, **sh**, or **x**.

I watch.   *Sarah watches.*

I catch.

I mix.

I rush.

I stretch.

The FINE Print   When the teacher calls the roll, you raise your hand and say, "Present." Present means you're here right now.
In grammar, tense means time. Present tense means the time right now.

© 2013 Handwriting Without Tears®

VERBS PRESENT (Tense)
You <u>surf</u>. He <u>surfs</u>.

CAPITAL
H

Verbs show action.   **surf**
Verbs show tense.   **You surf.** (present tense = now)
Verbs agree with subjects.   **You surf. Henry surfs.**

Trace the steps.   Write the letter.   ☐ Check H

H   H   H   H   H

       down   down   up + across   come back

Copy **He**. Do not connect **H** to the next letter.
Write sentences. Make the verbs agree. Add **-s.**

You surf.   He surfs.
You swim.
You float.
You wave.
You dive.

Copy **Henry** or write another name that starts with **H**.
Write sentences. Make the verbs agree. Add **-es** to verbs that end in **ch**, **sh**, or **o**.

You do chores.   Henry does chores.
You go out.
You watch movies.
You catch fish.
You rush home.

The FINE Print   In present tense, the verb changes to agree with 3rd person, singular subjects. (he, she, It)

            Can-Do Cursive **37**

VERBS PAST (Tense)
I danced.

Verbs show action. **dance**
Verbs show tense.   **I danced.** (past tense = It already happened.)
Regular verbs add **-d** or **-ed** to make the past tense.

Trace the steps.   Write the letter.   ☐ Check *I*

I   *(*   *(*   *I*   *I*   _____   _____
     curve up   down   big J-turn   end

Change these sentences to past tense.
Add **-ed**.

I report.   I talk.   I wait.

I reported.   _____   _____

For **e** endings, add **-d**.

I vote.   I skate.   I dance.

_____   _____   _____

Change **y** endings to **i**, and add **-ed**.

I carry.   I hurry.   I try.

_____   _____   _____

Double the last letter for vowel-consonant endings, then add **-ed**.

I snap.   I bat.   I skip.

_____   _____   _____

Is it a duck?
The 🦆 Test

Looks like a duck?	Y
Swims like a duck?	Y
Quacks like a duck?	Y
It's a duck!	

Is it a verb?
The VERB Test

Does it work with "to" in front? Yes, it's a verb!

to walk?	Y	to write?	____
to hair?	N	to door?	____
to run?	____	to read?	____
to elephant?	____	to window?	____

VERBS FUTURE (Tense)
She will skate.

Verbs show action. **skate**
Verbs show tense. **She will skate.** (future tense = It will happen, but it hasn't happened yet.)
All verbs use the helping verb **will** to make the future tense.

VERB   **WILL + VERB = FUTURE**

Write sentences with future tense verbs.

skate   *Nina will skate.*

run   _____

walk   _____

call   _____

CONTRACTIONS - APOSTROPHES

A contraction is a short form of two words.
An apostrophe substitutes for missing letters.

CONTRACTIONS			
I will	**I'll**	it will	**it'll**
you will	**you'll**	we will	**we'll**
he will	**he'll**	they will	**they'll**
she will	**she'll**	will not	**won't**

FUTURE WITH CONTRACTIONS

Change the words into contractions. Write below.

I will   *you will*   *he will*   *she will*

I'll   _____   _____   _____

it will   *we will*   *they will*   *will not*

_____   _____   _____   _____

Write a sentence about something you hope will happen in the future.

_____

_____

The FINE Print   When grammar teachers say "tense," they're not talking about tense muscles or being uptight. They're talking about verbs.
Present tense means now.
Past   tense means it already happened.
Future tense means it will happen.

CAPITALS
D G E L J Q

Trace the steps.

D | J   L   D   ☐ Check D

      down   J-turn   flip over   curve up + end

G   J   G   G   G   ☐ Check G

       curve up   top like e + i   down J-turn   end

E   C   E   ☐ Check E

      C in the air   C again
                     travel away

L   e   L   L   L   ☐ Check L

  start like e in the air   drop down   J-turn   flip over
                                          travel away

J   (J   J   J   ☐ Check J

       curve   straight down   J-turn   aim for corner
                                            travel away

Q   Q   Q   Q   or   Q   ☐ Check Q

    half heart   small turn   flip over
                          travel away

Copy the letters below. Do not connect.   Copy the letters. Connect.

Dd   Gg   Ee   Ll   Jj   Qq

The FINE Print   Some of the least used capitals, like **J** and **Q,** get the highest points in Scrabble®.

CAPITALIZATION RULES

CAP COLLECTION

Copy each capital next to the example.

a	B	C	D	E	F	G	
H	I	G	K	L	M	N	
O	P	Q	R	S	J	U	
V	W	X	Y	Z			

CAPITALIZATION RULES

Always capitalize the first word in a sentence and the pronoun **I**. Here are some other capitalization rules.

Capitalize: Complete the sentences.

Name of a person   *My name is* _____ .

Initials   *My initials are* _____ .

Days   *Today is* _____ .

Months   *My birthday is in* _____ .

Holidays   *My favorite holiday is* _____ .

Languages   *I speak* _____ .

Titles and names   *My teacher's name is* _____ .

Schools   *My school is* _____ .

Book titles   *My favorite book is* _____ .

First word of a quotation   *My friend said,"* _____ ."

Cities, towns, states, provinces   *I live in* _____ .

Rivers, lakes, and oceans   *The closest water is* _____ .

Write sentences about places you would like to visit. Using the capitalization rules above, see how many capitals you can include.

ADJECTIVES

happy, cheerful
hairy, bald

Adjectives describe nouns.
Adjectives tell how many, what kind, color, or condition.

SYNONYMS

Synonyms are words that have the same, or nearly the same meaning.
See the synonym pairs below.

Synonyms

Copy below the models.

happy   cheerful

elderly   old

Synonyms

angry   furious

large   huge

ANTONYMS

Antonyms are words that have the opposite, or nearly the opposite meaning. Here are some "hairy" antonyms. See the antonym pairs below.

Antonyms

Translate the printed adjectives into cursive.

hairy   bald

thick   thin

Antonyms

long   short

frizzy   straight

Draw hair.

© 2013 Handwriting Without Tears®

ADJECTIVES

Some adjectives describe just one thing. **cold** day
Comparative adjectives compare two things. **colder** day
Superlative adjectives compare three or more things. **coldest** day

ADJECTIVE	COMPARATIVE (-er) Write the comparative forms. Add **-er**.	SUPERLATIVE (-est) Write the superlative forms. Add **-est**.
cold	colder	coldest
few		
dark		
neat		

Change the **y** to **i** first.

friendly	friendlier	friendliest
messy		
sunny		
happy		

ADJECTIVE	"more" COMPARATIVE Write the comparative forms. Add more.	"most" SUPERLATIVE Write the comparative forms. Add most.
modern	more modern	most modern
stylish		
useful		
careful		

The FINE Print   Be careful of the **o + r** and **o + s** connections in *more* and *most*. _or_ _os_

PRONOUNS - SUBJECT CASE

1st, 2nd, 3rd Person

I, you, he, she, it
we, you, they

Pronouns take the place of nouns.
Subject pronouns take the place of subject nouns.
> **Joe** is drinking a milkshake.
> **He** is drinking a milkshake.

PERSON	SINGULAR - 1	PLURAL 2 or more
First	I	we
Second	you	you
Third	he, she, it	they

PRONOUN ASSISTANCE

RING FOR SERVICE

HEY! *I* AM THE FIRST PERSON.

YOU ARE THE SECOND PERSON.

HE IS THE THIRD PERSON.

JOE MALLETT

The FINE Print **Singular** nouns and pronouns name one. **boy/he**
Plural nouns and pronouns name two or more. **kids/they**
When teachers talk about **number**, they mean singular or plural.
When teachers talk about **person**, they mean first person, second person, or third person.
When teachers talk about **gender**, they mean masculine or feminine. **he/she**

PRONOUNS - OBJECT CASE

Object pronouns take the place of object nouns.

She called **Joe**.
She called **him**.

The subject pronoun does the action. **She**
The verb shows action. She **called**
The object pronoun receives the action. She called **him.**

SUBJECT PRONOUN → **VERB** → **OBJECT PRONOUN**

She and he → called → us.

SUBJECT PRONOUNS	VERBS	OBJECT PRONOUNS
I, you, he, she, we, they, he and I, she and I, he and she, you and I, you and he	asked, called, found, saw, praised, visited, called	me, you, him, her, us, them, him and her, her and him, you and me, you and her

Write your own sentences in **subject** → **verb** → **object** order.
Choose the subject pronouns, verbs, and object pronouns from the groups above.

1. _____

2. _____

3. _____

4. _____

5. _____

6. _____

7. _____

The FINE Print   Choose the pronoun by the job it does in the sentence.
If a pronoun is the **subject** of the sentence, use a **subject pronoun**.
If a pronoun is the **object** of a verb or preposition, use an **object pronoun**.

PRONOUNS - POSSESSIVE CASE

my, your, his, her our, your, their

Possessive pronouns show ownership. They take the place of possessive nouns.

Patrick's car	**Meagan's** car	**the car's** trunk	**Mike and Greg's** mom
his car	**her** car	**its** trunk	**their** mom

Give these possessive subject pronouns something to own. Choose from the list below or make up your own.

shoes	bike	party	friends	shirt	pizza	soda	money	present

my _____ your _____ his _____ her _____

its _____ our _____ your _____ their _____

These possessive object pronouns also show ownership. Fill in the blanks. Choose pronouns from the list below.

mine	yours	his	hers	ours	theirs

This bus is _____, but that bus is _____.

This book is _____, but that book is _____.

This pizza is _____, but the calzone is _____.

Three Little Kittens

Do you remember "Three Little Kittens?" Not only did they lose their mittens, they also lost their pronouns. Help Mother Goose get this rhyme right!

Fill in the missing pronouns. Choose pronouns from the list below.

we	you	they	our	your	their

Three little kittens, _____ lost their mittens,

And _____ began to cry, Oh, Mother Dear, _____ sadly fear,

_____ mittens _____ have lost. What! Lost _____ mittens!

_____ naughty kittens! Then _____ shall have no pie.

The FINE Print   Choosing the right pronouns is easy as pie if you know the job it does in the sentence. (**Whose** is also a possessive case pronoun.)

PRONOUN REVIEW

You've heard of suitcases, briefcases, and guitar cases.
The pronoun plane has landed. Here are the pronoun cases.

SUBJECT PRONOUN CASE

A **subject** case pronoun tells who the sentence is about: **I** get the case.

I	**we**
you	**you**
he, she, it	**they**

OBJECT PRONOUN CASE

An **object** case pronoun is the object of a verb: You watch **me**.

or

An **object** case pronoun is the object of a preposition.   This case is for **me**.

me	**us**
you	**you**
him, her, it	**them**

POSSESSIVE PRONOUN CASE

A **possessive case** pronoun owns something.   Is it **yours** or **mine**?
It's **my** case.

my, mine	**our, ours**
your, yours	**you, yours**
his, her, hers, its	**their, theirs**

Singular means one. To make singular nouns possessive, just add **'s**.

SINGLE PEOPLE

1. Make a list of eight people.
2. Start each name with a capital.   **Jose**
3. Add **'s**.   **Jose's**
4. Give each person a possession.   **Jose's gerbil**

1. *Jose's gerbil*   5. _____

2. _____   6. _____

3. _____   7. _____

4. _____   8. _____

Articles **a** or **an** go before singular nouns.
Use **a** before nouns that start with a consonant sound.   **a bird, a cat**
Use **an** before nouns that start with a vowel sound.   **an ant, an eagle**

SINGLE ANIMALS

1. Make a list of eight animals down the middle column.
2. Write **a** or **an** before each animal.   **an elephant**
3. Add **'s**.   **an elephant's**
4. Give each animal a possession.   **an elephant's trunk**

1. *an   elephant's   trunk*   Draw one of the animals.

2. _____ _____ _____

3. _____ _____ _____

4. _____ _____ _____

5. _____ _____ _____

6. _____ _____ _____

7. _____ _____ _____

8. _____ _____ _____

The FINE Print   **The** is a definite article. Use **the** before specific nouns. Use **the** before singular or plural nouns: **the** boy, **the** boys.

NOUNS - PLURAL POSSESSIVE

Add ' or 's

There are two ways to make plural nouns possessive.
1. Add 's to nouns that do not end in **s**.   **men** → **men's**
2. Add ' to nouns that end in **s**.   **ladies** → **ladies'**

COLUMN 1 Copy the nouns that **do not end in s**: Add 's	PLURAL NOUNS	COLUMN 2 Copy the nouns that **end in s**: Add '
women's	women	
	citizens	citizens'
	men	
	friends	
	kids	
	cattle	
	cows	
	children	
	ushers	
	cars	
	buses	
	geese	
	ladies	
	states	
	cities	

IRREGULAR VERBS

There are regular verbs and irregular verbs.
Regular verbs add **-d** or **-ed** to talk about the past.
I **walk**.   I **walked**.   I have **walked**.

Irregular verbs are rule breakers. They have their own forms.
I **give**.   I **gave**.   I have **given**.

Past participles are verb forms that use a helping "have" verb.

PRESENT	PAST	(have, has, had) + PAST PARTICIPLE
break	broke	broken
choose	chose	chosen
do	did	done
eat	ate	eaten
go	went	gone
give	gave	given
hide	hid	hidden
know	knew	known
leave	left	left
take	took	taken

have
has   +
had

Fill in the missing forms for each verb. Use the chart above if you need help.

	PRESENT	PAST	(have, has, or had) + PAST PARTICIPLE
1.	break	broke	have broken
2.	know		have
3.	do		have
4.	take		have
5.	choose		has
6.	go		has
7.	hide		has
8.	give		had
9.	leave		had
10.	eat		had

The FINE Print   Inside story: **ir** = not. **Ir**regular verbs are not regular. Look up irregular verbs in a dictionary to find their past tense and past participle forms. Many grammar books have irregular verb charts.

HELPING "have" VERBS

We have walked.

Have, has, had are helping "**have**" verbs.
A helping **have** verb + past participle = perfect verb tense.
Perfect verb tenses can happen in the present, in the past, and in the future.

HEY, WHAT MAKES THEM PERFECT?

PRESENT PERFECT
have (or has) + past participle

Copy below the models.

We have walked for miles.

They have taken a break.

Copy.

He has eaten lunch.   She has left town.

PAST PERFECT
had + past participle

Copy.

Joe had bought two tickets.

FUTURE PERFECT
will have + past participle

Copy.

I will have finished by noon.

☐ Check Sentence

The FINE Print   What makes a perfect tense? The words **have, has, had** tell you it's a perfect tense.
"Perfect" usually has a different meaning. This is just the "English grammar" use of the word "perfect."

© 2013 Handwriting Without Tears®

Can-Do Cursive **51**

LINKING VERBS

LINKING "be" VERBS

Linking "be" verbs don't act; they don't even help other verbs.
Linking verbs work alone. They make a statement or tell it like it is: **Dr. Less is nice**.

LINKING "sensory" VERBS

Linking "sensory" verbs tell how things look, feel, sound, taste, or smell. They link the sentence together.
He **looks** happy. I **feel** bad. It **sounds** great. My burrito **tastes** good. Your socks **smell** awful.

SUBJECT →	LINKING VERB →	WORD OR PHRASE (ADJECTIVE)

Make up sentences using linking verbs. Don't forget the punctuation.

1. _The burrito_ → _tastes_ → _good._

2. _____ _are_ _____

3. _____ _seems_ _____

4. _____ _is_ _____

5. _____ _looks_ _____

6. _____ _sounds_ _____

Write about your favorite food. What does it look like? How does it taste? What is the smell?

© 2013 Handwriting Without Tears®

HELPING "be" VERBS

The "**be**" verbs aren't just linking verbs. They can also be helping verbs.
The helping "be" verbs include **am**, **is**, **are**, **was**, **were**, **will be**, **has been**.
Present participles are the **ing** form of the verb. **eat** → **eating**
Helping "**be**" verbs and present participles work together. I **am eating**. I **was eating.** I **will be eating.**

PRESENT PARTICIPLES = PLAIN VERB + ing

Write present participles.

eat + ing   = _____   wait + ing   = _____

cook + ing = _____   paint + ing = _____

talk + ing   = _____   sail + ing   = _____

CONTRACTIONS & APOSTROPHES

Remember contractions? They're short forms of two words. Letters are left out. An apostrophe takes the place of the missing letters.

CONTRACTIONS	
I am	**I'm**
you are	**you're**
she is	**she's**
he is	**he's**
it is	**it's**
we are	**we're**
you are	**you're**
they are	**they're**

Rewrite the sentences with contractions.

I am thinking.   I'm thinking.

You are cooking.   _____

She is talking.   _____

He is waiting.   _____

It is raining.   _____

We are performing.   _____

You are singing.   _____

☐ Check Sentence

ADVERBS

Adverbs tell when, how often, where, why, and how.

Adverbs usually describe verbs.   The dog **never** bites.
Adverbs sometimes describe other adverbs.   She barked **very** loudly.
Adverbs occasionally describe adjectives.   She's a **really** good dog.

HOW OFTEN?

never	rarely	sometimes	usually	always

These adverbs tell how often, from never to always.
Answer these questions with complete sentences. Choose from the adverbs above. Stop with a period.

How often do you

. . . eat chicken?   I sometimes eat chicken.

. . . drink milk?   I

. . . make your bed?   I

. . . do the dishes?   I

. . . read the comics?   I

. . . go fishing?   I

. . . read mysteries?   I

☐ Check Sentence

Write about your everyday life. What do you always do? What do you never do?

_____

_____

_____

_____

Adverbs tell how someone acts or does something.
Many adverbs end in **-ly**.

ANTONYMS

An antonym is a word that means the opposite.
Here are pairs of antonyms that are adverbs.

Antonyms

Copy one word of each pair. It's your choice.

bravely	fearfully
deliberately	accidentally
loudly	quietly
roughly	tenderly

Antonyms

carefully	carelessly
formally	informally
quickly	slowly
well	poorly

Adverbs tell how someone does something.
Do you play a sport or musical instrument? Write about something you do using an adverb that ends in **-ly**.

_____

_____

_____

_____

The FINE Print   Not all words that end in **-ly** are adverbs. Friendly, ugly, costly, and others are adjectives. Check a dictionary to be sure.

Can-Do Cursive **55**

PREPOSITIONS

before, after, on, off, over, under . .

Prepositions show position or time.
Copy the prepositions below the models.

above	before	up	over	in
below	after	down	under	out
during	inside	on	between	around
since	outside	off	beside	through

GOING ON A PREPOSITION HUNT

Go on a bear hunt and a preposition hunt. Underline the prepositions you find in "Going on a Bear Hunt."
Use the list above for clues.

GOING ON A BEAR HUNT

We're going on a bear hunt,
We're gonna catch a big one,
I'm not afraid! Are you? Not me!

I see tall grass,
Can't go over it,
Let's go through it.

I see a bridge,
Can't go around it,
Let's go over it.

I see a lake,
Can't go over it,
Can't go under it,
Let's swim.

I see a tree,
Can't go over it,
Can't go under it,
Let's go up it,
I don't see any bears,
Let's go down.

I see a swamp,
Can't go over it,
Can't go under it,
Let's go through it.

I see a cave,
Can't go over it,
Can't go under it,
Let's go in.
I see two eyes, I see two ears,
I see a nose, I see a mouth,
Yikes! It's a bear!
Let's get out of here.

The FINE Print   Be careful of the **v + e** and **b + e** connections in above and before.   ve   be

© 2013 Handwriting Without Tears®

PREPOSITIONAL PHRASES

Over the rainbow is not a sentence.
Over the rainbow is a phrase.
Over the rainbow starts with a preposition.
Over the rainbow is a prepositional phrase.

A phrase is a group of related words.
A phrase has a subject or a verb, but not both.
Prepositional phrases start with a preposition.

Make up prepositional phrases. Add an article (**a**, **an**, or **the**) and a noun.

PREPOSITION	ARTICLE	NOUN
over	the	rainbow
under		
behind		
during		
beside		
on		
into		
inside		
around		

PREPOSITIONAL PHRASES IN SENTENCES

Translate the printed sentences into cursive.

My   hamster   ran   under   the   bed.

After   the   game,   we   raced   home.

☐ Check Sentence

The FINE Print   **After the game** is an introductory phrase. Use a comma after an introductory phrase.

CONJUNCTIONS

Conjunctions are words that join words, phrases, or clauses.

COMPOUND SENTENCES

Two sentences joined = one compound sentence.
There are two ways to make compound sentences:
      1. Use a comma and a conjunction. **, and**   **, or**   **, but**
      2. Use a semicolon. **;**

COMMA and CONJUNCTION
, and

Let's get ready to write compound sentences with commas and conjunctions.   **, or**

, but

Copy the commas and conjunctions below the models:

  , and   , or   , but   , so   , yet   , for   , nor

Use a comma and a conjunction to join the sentences. See the example below.

      Mr. Wright has a new car.   Mr. Case has an old car.
      Mr. Wright has a new car**, but** Mr. Case has an old car.

                      comma, conjunction

The boys can stay.   They must leave soon.

Ann sings.   Tom plays the piano.

SEMICOLON ;

Use a semicolon to join the sentences. See the example below.

         Dr. Less writes books. Her friend illustrates them.
         Dr. Less writes books**;** her friend illustrates them.

            semicolon   lowercase **h**

We went to Ohio.   They went to Alberta.

The FINE Print   The root **semi** = half, so a semicolon (**;**) is half a colon (**:**). Use semicolons to link related ideas.

ABBREVIATIONS

Abbreviations are shortened words. Use a period after an abbreviation. **Doctor → Dr.**

TITLES
Copy these abbreviations below the models.

Dr. *Mr.* *Mrs.* *Ms.*

ABBREVIATE THE DAYS
Abbreviate the days of the week. Find the answers upside down.

Monday *Tuesday* *Wednesday* *Thursday*

Friday *Saturday* *Sunday*

Mon. *Tue.* *Wed.* *Thur.* *Fri.* *Sat.* *Sun.*

MONTHS
May, June, and July are short. They are not abbreviated and do not use periods. Copy below.

Jan. *Feb.* *Mar.* *Apr.*

Aug. *Sept.* *Oct.* *Nov.* *Dec.*

ABBREVIATE THE WORDS
Change these words into abbreviations.

Doctor *Monday* *March* *December* *August*

PUNCTUATION

Look at all the places a comma should be.
- In a series
- After an introductory clause
- Before conjunctions used to separate clauses
- Before quoting a speaker
- Between a city and a state
- In a date, between the day and the year

Copy below the models. Don't forget any commas!

Commas – in a series

keys, socket wrench, screwdriver, pump

Commas – after an introductory clause

When he finished the course,

Comma – before conjunctions used to separate clauses

He wants a new bike, but he can't afford one.

Comma – before quoting a speaker

Scottie said,   *Jessica said,*

Comma – between a city and a state

Tulsa, Oklahoma   *Baltimore, Maryland*

Commas – in dates, between the day and the year

Feb. 6, 2013   *Oct. 31, 2013*

QUOTATIONS

Quotation marks show someone's exact words.
Learn to write quotations from the comics. Here are two ways to write quotations.

Mr. Case said, "My car is a lemon."

or

"My car is a lemon," said Mr. Case.

Mr. Wright yelled, "Go, go, go!"

or

"Go, go, go!" yelled Mr Wright.

Mrs. New asked, "Do you need help?"

or

"Do you need help?" asked Mrs. New.

Your choice. Copy three of the quotations above, or copy quotations from your favorite comic strip.

1. _____

2. _____

3. _____

TWO WAYS TO WRITE QUOTATIONS

1 - The NAME comes first.
Mr. Case said, "My car is a lemon."

2 - The QUOTE comes first.
"My car is a lemon," said Mr. Case.

Make up a comic strip. Draw characters and give them quote bubbles. Fill in the bubbles with what the characters say.

© 2013 Handwriting Without Tears®

Can-Do Cursive **61**

INTERJECTIONS!

Interjections are not sentences. Interjections are just one or two words that express feelings.

1. Strong interjections end with an exclamation point.
   Yikes!   Rats!   Whew!   Gosh!   Good grief!

2. A comma follows mild interjections.
   Hey, I'm next.   **Oh**, I understand.   **Well**, that's over.   **Hmm**, let's go.

HEY, WHAT'S WITH THE TOGA?

Make up some interjections for these situations.

The doctor just gave you a shot. _____

Someone just cut ahead of you in line. _____

You won the bike race. _____

You came in last. _____

The pool water is ice cold. _____

Friends surprise you with a big cake. _____

CURSIVE WITH GREEK & LATIN

In the ancient world, Greek and Latin were widely spoken.
The Romans spoke Latin. People in Greece spoke Greek. They still do.
This magnified (**magn** = big) view shows Greece and Italy (and Rome).

THIS IS A HEMISPHERE.
HEMI = HALF
SPHERE = GLOBE, BALL

HEY, IT'S EASY!

More than 60 percent of English words come from Greek and Latin. Knowing a little Greek and Latin is like knowing a secret code. You have an easy way to figure out words.

GREEK & LATIN Copy in cursive.	MEANING	ENGLISH WORDS
ort _____	= carry	export, portable, deport, portfolio
micro _____	= small	microscope, microwave, microchip
ology _____	= study of	psychology, biology, zoology

capital →
column →

The FINE Print   A column is a tall pillar that supports a building or a statue. The top of a column is called a capital.

GETTING TO THE ROOT OF THINGS

PREFIXES come first—**preview, return**. Copy the prefixes.

pre

re

_____ = before

_____ = again

ROOTS are main word parts—**aquatic, tricycle**. Copy the roots.

aqua

cycl

_____ = water

_____ = circle, wheel

SUFFIXES come after roots—**aquarium, solidify**. Copy the suffixes.

arium

ify

_____ = place for

_____ = to make

BUILDING WORDS WITH PREFIXES

The prefix pre = before.

Copy pre.

Combine the parts to make a new word.

(pre) + dict = _____

(___) + pare = _____

(___) + vent = _____

The prefix re = again.

Copy re.

Combine the parts to make a new word.

(re) + form = _____

(___) + fund = _____

(___) + read = _____

The FINE Print   There are three styles of Greek capitals. The capitals at the top of this page are Ionic capitals. They look like a scroll.

GROWING WORDS

GROWING WORDS WITH ROOTS

The root _port_ = carry.

Copy _port_.   Combine the parts to make a new word.

trans + (port) = transport

ex + (_____) = _____

(_____) + folio = _____

(_____) + able = _____

The root _scope_ = look at.

Copy _scope_.   Combine the parts to make a new word.

tele + (scope) = _____

peri + (_____) = _____

kaleido + (_____) = _____

BUILDING WORDS WITH SUFFIXES

The suffix _meter_ = measure.

Copy _meter_.   Combine the parts to make a new word.

thermo + (meter) = _____

peri + (_____) = _____

baro + (_____) = _____

The suffix _ify_ = to make.

Copy _ify_.   Combine the parts to make a new word.

solid + (ify) = _____

liqu + (_____) = _____

ampl + (_____) = _____

The FINE Print   The capitals on this page are Corinthian capitals. They have leaves.

WORD DETECTIVES

Doric capital →

GREEK ROOTS
Copy.

sphere _____   meter _____   therm _____   magn _____

_____   _____   _____   _____

GUESSING GREEK
Look at the root and the clue words that use the root. Then guess what the root means. Find the answers upside down.

<u>sphere</u> – hemisphere, spherical, atmosphere, stratosphere

I guess sphere means _____

<u>meter</u> – speedometer, barometer, thermometer, diameter

I guess meter means _____

<u>therm</u> – thermal, thermos, thermometer, thermostat

I guess therm means _____

<u>magn</u> – magnify, magnificent, magnanimous, magnification

I guess magn means _____

sphere = ball, meter = measure, therm = heat, magn = large

Draw a picture of the underlined word and then write the definition:

A <u>magnifying</u> glass is _____

A <u>thermometer</u> is _____

The FINE Print   The capitals on this page are Doric capitals.

© 2013 Handwriting Without Tears®

WORD DETECTIVES

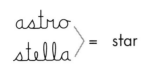

Here are more familiar Greek and Latin roots:

astro
stella ⟩ = star

con = together

cycl = wheel, circle

graph = write, draw

micro = small

naut = sailor

octo = eight

photo = light

ped
pod ⟩ = foot

scope = look at

tri = three

Decode the words below by writing the meaning of their roots.

tricycle = <u>three</u> + <u>wheels</u>

microscope = _____ + _____

astronaut = _____ + _____

photograph = _____ + _____

tripod = _____ + _____

constellation = _____ + _____

(Tip: The suffix **-tion** = state of, condition)

Now draw pictures of some of the things listed on the page.

Greek and Latin help you decipher big science words:

ornithology	biology	paleontology	geology	zoology	entomology

bio = life   *entomon* = insect   *ology* = study of

ge = earth   *ornith* = bird   *ologist* = one who studies

mar = sea   *zo* = animal

paleo = old

Choose from the following list to match the scientists to what they study. Write your answers in cursive.

biologist	entomologist	geologist	~~marine biologist~~	ornithologist	paleontologist	zoologist

marine biologist   sea life

birds

insects

structure of the earth

living things

old life forms and fossils

animals

DID YOU SEE THAT ORNITHOLOGIST WATCHING US?

The FINE Print   The suffix **-ist** = an expert in. Do you know any other **-ist** experts? What about an anthropologist, a scientist, or an astrophysicist?

Knowing roots helps you make smart guesses about words.
Dig into the root *micro*.

microscope   **micro**wave   **micro**meter

What does *micro* mean? _____

What is a micrometer? Take a guess.

___small bug   ___device for small measurements   ___small parking meter

Guess what these things are. Write your guesses in cursive. Find the answers upside down.

microcomputer   =   _____

microscope   =   _____

microwave   =   _____

micrometer = device for making small measurements, microcomputer = small computer, microscope = instrument to see small things, microwave = small electromagnetic wave used in cooking

THINK BIG!

magn = great, big, large   *opus* = work   *charta* = document

Complete these sentences. Choose from the words below. The roots will help you. Remember your periods.

| magnify | magnificent | magnitude | Magna Carta | magnum opus |

To make larger is to

England's 1215 document is the

Something impressive or beautiful is

The size or importance of something is

A great, often artistic work is a

The FINE Print   Magna Carta is also written Magna Charta. Magnet and magnolia come from different roots, not **magn** = big.

I	1	_umi_ – unicycle, uniform, unit
II	2	_bi_ – bicycle, biceps, bilingual
III	3	_tri_ – tricycle, triple, triangle, triatholon
IV	4	_quad, tetra_ – quadriceps, quadruplets, tetrology
V	5	_quin, penta_ – quintuplets, quintet, pentagon, pentathlon
VI	6	_sex, hex_ – sextet, hexagon
VII	7	_sept_ – septagon
VIII	8	_oct, octo_ – octopus, octagon, octave
IX	9	_novem_
X	10	_dec, decem, deca_ – decade, decimal
L	50	_quinquaginta_
C	100	_cent_ – century, centennial, cent

Finish the sentences. Find clues above. Find the answers upside down.

II _A bicycle has_

III _A tricycle has_

V _The pentagon has_

C _A century has_

two wheels, three wheels, five sides, 100 years

Copy these roots. They help with metric words.

deci

_____ = tenth

centi

_____ = hundredth

milli

_____ = thousandth

meter

_____ = unit of measure

Copy these metric words.

decimeter

1/10th of a meter

centimeter

1/100th of a meter

millimeter

1/1000th of a meter

The FINE Print   With September our ninth month, you'd think that **sept** meant nine. It doesn't. On the Roman calendar, September was the seventh month; October the eighth; November the ninth; and December the tenth month. We use a different calendar now.

MATH WORDS MADE EASY!

friends, Romans, countrymen, step right up for the inside story on math words.
Know the roots. Presto! Know the meanings.

angul $\Big\}$ = angle
gon

hex = six
iso = equal
oct = eight
parallelos = parallel
penta = five
poly = many
rect = right
tri = three

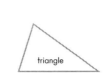

TRIANGLES have three sides and three angles.

Copy these roots and meanings.

tri = three   gon = angle   iso = equal   rect = right

_____   _____   _____   _____

Copy.

triangle △   right triangle ◺   isosceles triangle △

_____   _____   _____

RECTANGLES have four sides and four right angles.

SQUARES have four equal sides and four right angles.

Copy.

rect = right   90°   rectangles ☐☐   square ☐

_____   _____   _____

OTHER SHAPES

Write the number of sides beside each shape. Copy the words.

pentagon = 5   hexagon = ___   octagon = ___   triangle = ___

_____   _____   _____   _____

The FINE Print   Rect = right. Right angles are corner angles, like the corner of this page or a printed **L**.

HEAD TO TOE

GREEK

cephal = head
rhino = nose
odont = tooth
stetho = chest
derm = skin
dactyl = finger, toe
pod = foot

LATIN

capit = head
cardi = heart
dent = tooth
pulman = lung
manu = hand
digit = finger, toe
ped = foot

BONUS ROOT ortho = straight (He's standing straight and he's got straight teeth!)

Copy these English words that are based on Greek or Latin roots.

rhinoceros   manual   digital

_____   _____   _____

dentures   pedestrian   stethoscope

_____   _____   _____

Copy the doctors.

dermatologist   podiatrist   cardiologist   orthodontist

_____   _____   _____   _____

What body part do the doctors take care of? Fill in the blanks and end each sentence with a period.

A dermatologist takes care of the _____

A podiatrist takes care of the _____

A cardiologist takes care of the _____

An orthodontist straightens the _____

The FINE Print   Many medical and scientific terms come from these roots. Ask your parents about these and other medical specialists.
A pediatrician takes care of children, not feet!

SOUNDS ALL AROUND

Check out these clues:

audio	=	hear, hearing	*meter*	=	device for measuring
audit	=	hear, hearing	*micro*	=	small
caco	=	bad	*orium*	=	place for
eu	=	good	*phon*	=	sound
mega	=	big	*tele*	=	far

WHAT IS IT?

Fill in the blanks with one of the cursive answers below.

telephone	*cacophony*	*auditorium*	*phonics*

A big place to see and hear performances: _____

A sound that's awful, harsh, and off-key: _____

It rings: _____

Letter and word sounds: _____

microphone	*megaphone*	*euphonious*	*audiometer*

A device for measuring hearing: _____

Pleasant-sounding to the ear: _____

Singers hold me: _____

Cheerleaders use it to make their voices loud: _____

Write a sentence with one of the sound words.

_____

_____

VAST SEAS

Sail the seas with Greek and Latin roots.
Copy the cursive roots below.

aqua = water

hydro = water

fire **hydra**nt

nav = ship

sub = under

mar = sea

endo = inner

exo = outer

skeleto = skeleton

peri = around

scope = look at

Fill in the blanks. Translate the printed answer into cursive.

| endoskeleton | exoskeleton | marine | navy | periscope | submarine |

Look through the _____ on our yellow _____
            periscope   submarine

I'm a lobster. I have an _____.
                             exoskeleton

I'm a shark. I have an _____.
                         endoskeleton

A sailor has enlisted in the _____.
                             navy

I work on coral reefs. I'm studying _____ life.
                             marine

Write a watery sentence or two.

_____

_____

STARRY SKIES

e night sky is filled with stars. Constellations are groups of stars.

con = together **stella** = star **canis** = dog **ursa** = bear **major** = big

rsa Major = The Big Bear

Copy these sentences.

The Big Dipper is part of Ursa Major.

Sirius is the brightest star.

Sirius is part of Canis Major.

nis Major = The Big Dog

LANETS

mnemonic helps you remember something. Use this mnemonic for the order of the planets:

"**M**y **V**ery **E**xcellent **M**other **J**ust **S**erved **U**s **N**oodles!"

rite the planet names in order from the sun.

Earth	Jupiter	Mars	Mercury	Neptune	Saturn	Uranus	Venus

Mercury	*J*
V	*S*
E	*U*
m	*n*

e FINE Print   Cool roots: **astro** = star, **naut** = sailor. Cool meaning: Astronauts are star sailors! Think of S.U.N. to remember the three planets that are the farthest from the sun.

You walk on terra firm.

Copy these earth words below the model.

In Latin, **terra** = earth, land

firma = solid

territory

terrarium

terrain

_____

_____

_____

geography

geology

geoscience

_____

_____

_____

Botany is the study of plants. Some botany roots:

chloro = green   **hydro** = water   **stella** = star

epi = on, upon   **ology** = study of   **trop** = turn

ge = earth   **phyll** = leaf   **zo** = animal

helio = sun   **phyt** = plant

Fill in the blanks with the meanings of the roots. See how the root meanings compare with the actual definition.

WORD	ROOT MEANINGS		ACTUAL DEFINITIO
chlorophyll =	*green*	+ *leaf*	A green substance in plants
epiphyte =	_____	+ _____	A plant that grows on other plants
geology =	_____	+ _____	The study of Earth's soil and rock lay▸
hydrology =	_____	+ _____	The study of water
heliotropic =	_____	+ _____	Turning toward the sun
zoology =	_____	+ _____	Study of animals
stellaria =	_____		Small white flowers shaped like stars

Did you ever do a science project about plants?

Describe your project.

_____

_____

The FINE Print   Here's a great word: **zoophyte**. What could an "animal plant" be? Zoophytes are animals that look like plants — sea anemones, corals, and sponges, for instance. (They're invertebrates—no backbone: **in** = not + **verebra** = joint.)

FALSE CLUES : "TRI" AGAIN!

Sometimes you'll spot what looks like a Greek or Latin clue, but it won't be a true clue. Take **tri,** for example. Don't be tricked. Not all words with **tri** are related to the root **tri,** meaning three.

These words are **NOT related to the prefix tri.**
Translate these printed words into cursive.

tribe   trick   trim   trip

tribe

These words are **related to the prefix tri.**
Translate these printed words into cursive.

triangle   triplicate   tricycle

triangle

triceratops   tripod   triplets

trilogy   trident   trio

Draw three pictures of **tri** words.

TRY THIS - TRANSLATE

Grab your togas and laurel wreaths!
Translate these Greek and Latin roots. Write your answers in cursive. Find the answers upside down.

GREEK/LATIN	ENGLISH		GREEK/LATIN	ENGLISH
1. aqua, hydro	= _____		16. manu	= _____
2. astro, stella	= _____		17. meter	= _____
3. canis	= _____		18. micro	= _____
4. cardi	= _____		19. milli	= _____
5. capit, cephal	= _____		20. octo	= _____
6. con	= _____		21. paleo	= _____
7. dactyl, digit	= _____		22. ped, pod	= _____
8. dent	= _____		23. phon, son	= _____
9. derm	= _____		24. phyt	= _____
10. eu	= _____		25. poly	= _____
11. ge	= _____		26. port	= _____
12. gon, angul	= _____		27. pre	= _____
13. helio	= _____		28. tele	= _____
14. iso	= _____		29. terra	= _____
15. magn, mega	= _____		30. trop	= _____

1. water
2. star
3. dog
4. heart
5. head
6. with, together
7. finger, toe
8. tooth
9. skin
10. good
11. earth
12. angle
13. sun
14. equal
15. big
16. hand
17. measure
18. small
19. thousand
20. eight
21. old
22. foot
23. sound
24. plant
25. many
26. carry
27. before
28. far
29. earth, land
30. turn, change

A **angul, gon** = angle 71, 78
aqua, hydr, hydro = water 64, 74, 76, 78
arium, orium = place for 64, 73
astro, stella = star 67, 75, 76, 78
audit, audio = hear, hearing 73

B **baro** = pressure 65
bi = two 70
bio = life 68

C **caco** = bad 73
canis = dog 75, 78
capit, cephal = head 72, 78
cent = hundred 70
centi = hundredth 70
cephal, capit = head 72, 78
charta = document 69
chloro = green 76
con = together, with 67, 75, 78
cycl = circle, wheel 64, 67

D **dactyl, digit** = toe, finger 72, 78
dec, decem, deca = ten 70
deci = tenth 70
dent, odon, odont = tooth 72, 78
derm = skin 72, 78
digit, dactyl = toe, finger 72, 78
endo = inner 74
entomon = insect 68

E **epi** = on, upon 76
eu = well, good 73, 78
ex = out of 65
exo = outer 74
firma = solid 76

F **folio, phyll** = sheet, leaf 65, 76

G **ge, terra** = earth, land 68, 76, 78
gon, angul = angle 71, 78
graph = write, draw 67

H **helio** = sun 76, 78
hemi = half 63
hex, sex = six 70, 71
hydr, hydro, aqua = water 64, 74, 76, 78

I **-ify** = to make 64, 65
in = not 76
iso = equal 71, 78
-ist = expert in 68

M **magn, major, mega** = big, great, large 63, 66, 69, 73, 75, 78
manu = hand 72, 78
mar = sea 68, 74
meter = measure, device for measuring, unit of measure 65, 66, 70, 73, 78
micro = small 63, 67, 69, 73, 78
milli = thousandth 70, 78

N **naut** = sailor 67, 75
nav = ship 74
novem = nine 70

O **oct, octo** = eight 67, 70, 71, 78
odon, odont, dent = tooth 72, 78
ologist = one who studies 68
ology = study of 63, 68, 76
opus = work 69
orium, arium = place for 64, 73
ornith = bird 68
ortho = straight 72

P **paleo** = old 68, 78
parallelos = parallel 71
ped, pod = foot 67, 72, 78
penta, quin = five 70, 71
peri = around 65, 74
phyt = plant 76, 76
phon, son = sound 73, 78
photo = light 67
phyll, folio = leaf 65, 76
phyt = plant 76, 78
pod, ped = foot 67, 72, 78
poly = many 71, 78
port = carry 63, 65, 78
pre = before 64, 78
pulmon = lung 72

Q **quad, tetra** = four 70
quin, penta = five 70, 71
quinquaginta = fifty 70

R **re** = again 64
rect = right 71
rhino = nose 72

S **scope** = look at 65, 67, 74
semi = half 58
sept = seven 70
sex, hex = six 70
skeleto = skeleton 74
son, phon = sound 73, 78
sphere (from sphaîra) = ball, globe 63, 66
stella, astro = star 67, 75, 76, 78
stetho = chest 72
sub = under 74

T **tele** = far 65, 73, 78
terra, ge, geo = earth, land 68, 76, 78
tetra, quad = four 70
-tion = state of, condition 67
therm, thermo = heat 65, 66
trans = across 65
tri = three 67, 70, 71, 77
trop = turn 76, 78

U **uni** = one 70
ursa = bear 75

V **vertebra** = joint 76

Z **zo** = animal 68, 76

Wow! What a start on Greek and Latin word roots! You're on your way to becoming great word decoders. Try these: endoderm, pulmonologist, mariner, decade, epidermis, microbiology . . . you get the idea! Keep exploring. You've found the key to figuring out new words.

Can-Do Cursive

CURSIVE & THE WRITER'S NOTEBOOK

These famous writers welcome you to The Writer's Notebook.
Do you recognize any of them?

Emily Dickinson wrote poetry.
Frederick Douglass wrote an autobiography.
Anne Frank wrote a diary.
William Shakespeare wrote plays.
Mark Twain wrote short stories.

Now you are the writer!
In this section, you will be writing on notebook paper.

Your picture here

DETAILS, DETAILS

SPECIFIC DETAILS

For readers to see what you have in mind, use specific words instead of general words.

Write specific words.

sport → *baseball*   toy →

dog →   flower →

lunch →   bird →

insect →   car →

SENSORY DETAILS

Make your writing come alive with sensory details.
Tell what readers would see, hear, smell, taste, or touch.

Choose a setting:
1. Spaceship   2. Circus   3. Beach

Setting:

Describe what your reader will:

See:

Hear:

Smell:

Taste:

Touch:

PARAGRAPHS

Keep your paragraphs organized and structured:
1. Tell your reader what you're going to write about. This becomes the topic sentence.
2. Say it. Give supporting facts, details, and thoughts about your topic sentence.
3. Tell your reader what you said. Restate the idea from the topic sentence using different words.

Plan your paragraph.

My topic is:

Thoughts, facts, or details to include:

Write a draft.

1. Topic sentence:

2. Say it.

3. Restate the topic sentence in different words.

PARAGRAPHS

Now, it's time to write your own paragraph. Make sure you have a topic sentence. Don't forget the supporting facts and details. Finish it by restating the topic. Indent to start.

Write your paragraph.

DIARY OR JOURNAL NOTES

Anne Frank died in a concentration camp during World War II. After her death, her father found and published her diary. A diary is a personal book for daily writing. Usually diaries are private. You can buy a blank book for writing your daily thoughts and experiences.

A journal is also for personal, regular writing. Journals help people remember the details of special times or trips. Teachers often have students write in a journal at school. Journal writing develops your ability to observe, reflect, and write well.

Anne Frank
1929–1945

Write about your life today and about your thoughts.

Today's Date:

Thoughts and experiences:

AUTOBIOGRAPHY NOTES

If you write about your own life, it's an autobiography. Frederick Douglass wrote passionately about growing up as a slave, secretly learning to read and write, and finally becoming a free man.

To write an autobiography, you need:

1. Yourself
2. Places in your life
3. People in your life
4. Events in your life

Frederick Douglass
1818–1895

Write notes for your autobiography.

1. Yourself:

2. Places in your life:

3. People in your life:

4. Events in your life:

Use these notes to write a one-page autobiography.
Use a separate piece of paper.

LETTER WRITING

Friendly letters and notes are organized from top to bottom: Date, Greeting, Body, Closing, and Signature. Each part begins on a new line. Dates are at the top right. Greetings begin at the left margin. The body or message is indented like a paragraph. The closing and signature are centered.

DATES
Fill in the year. Copy the dates.

Jan. 1, 201   Feb. 1, 201   Mar. 1, 201

Apr. 1, 201   May 1, 201   June 1, 201

July 1, 201   Aug. 1, 201   Sept. 1, 201

Oct. 1, 201   Nov. 1, 201   Dec. 1, 201

GREETINGS
Copy.

Dear Aunt Alice,   Mr.   Mrs.   Ms.

CLOSINGS
Copy.

Sincerely,   Thank you,   Yours,   Love,

THANK YOU NOTES

Write a thank you letter. Organize your letter like this.

Date
Month Day, Year

Greeting
Dear _____ ,

Body
Say thank you and tell how much you appreciate the gift or help. Mention what it is or what they did. Add details to make it more personal.

Use a comma:
1. After the day of the month
2. After the greeting
3. After the closing

Closing
Sincerely, Thank you, or Love,

Signature

POETRY

Emily Dickinson
1830–1886

Emily Dickinson wrote poetry. There are many kinds of poems. Some rhyme, some don't. Some have a pattern, some don't. Try different types.

Haiku is a three line, 17-syllable poem of Japanese origin that doesn't rhyme. Haiku paints a picture or expresses a feeling.

School Starts

Pencil sharpened, paper fresh and clean,
Ideas swirl in my mind,
I write.

Beach

The ocean waves crashing,
Seagulls flying high above,
The sand is hot.

Try writing a Haiku.

1st line:

2nd line:

3rd line:

Now, it's time to write a different kind of poem. Pick a favorite person, sport, or season. Write the word vertically, one letter per line. Then, write a poem about your choice, starting each line with the letter listed.

PLAY NOTES

William Shakespeare
1564–1616

Shakespeare wrote plays. To write a play, you need:
1. Setting
2. Time
3. Characters
4. Plot

Write notes for a play.

1. Describe your setting.
   Where?

2. When?

3. Describe your main character.
   Age:
   Name:
   Traits:
   Interests:

4. Give ideas for your plot.
   On stage is:
   Tell what happens:

What happens next? It's up to you.

CHARACTER SKETCHES

Jef Mallett, the cartoonist, made sketches for the characters in this book. These sketches helped him decide what the final characters would look like.

Make up a character.

Name:

Age:

Sketch your characte

Describe things about your character's appearance.

Size:

Hair:

Clothing:

Describe some other things about your character.

Family:

Pets:

School or work:

Hobbies:

Write a sentence about what makes your character interesting.

CHARACTER SKETCHES

Here is Jef's sketch of Milk Shake Guy. See how the sketch became the final character.

Make up another character.

Name:

Age:

What does your character look like?

Size:

Hair:

Clothing:

Sketch your character.

Tell more about your character.

Family:

Pets:

School or work:

Hobbies:

Adventures:

Make up a comic strip. Draw characters and give them quote bubbles. Fill in the bubbles with what the characters say.
Use a blank sheet of paper.

SHORT STORY NOTES

Mark Twain wrote articles, short stories, and novels. One of his short stories was "The Celebrated Jumping Frog of Calaveras County." To write a short story, focus on one event. Make the event be funny, sad, dramatic, or scary.

Write notes for your short story.

Title:

Setting:

Mark Twain
1835–1910

Event:

Time:

Characters:

What happens in your story? It's up to you. Use your notes to write a one page story in cursive on a separate sheet of paper.

BOOK CASE NOTES

This is not a book report. These are Book CASE Notes.

Cover   Write the title of the book.
Author Write the author's name.
Start   Copy the first sentence of the book.
End   Copy the last sentence of the book.

For the title, be sure to capitalize the first, last, and important words.

Pick out a book and make your Book CASE Notes.

Sketch the cover.

Cover title:

Author's name:

Starting sentence:

Ending sentence:

BOOK CASE NOTES

Book CASE Notes are great for writing practice. They review both lowercase and capital letters. Stretch this activity for favorite books by telling what happened in the middle. The more you read, the stronger your writing will be!

Pick out a book and make your Book CASE Notes. This time, include what happened in the middle.

Cover title:

Author's name:

Starting sentence:

Sketch the cover.

Middle:

Ending sentence: